# ANIMAL FAMILIES

# Dolphins

angus

This edition published in 2004
by Angus Books Ltd
12 Ravensbury Terrace
London SW18 4RL

ISBN 1-904594-56-5

FOR BROWN PARTWORKS LIMITED
*Author:* Bridget Giles
*Consultant:* Dr. Adrian Seymour
*Project editor:* Tim Harris
*Managing editor:* Anne O'Daly
*Picture research:* Adrian Bentley
*Index:* Margaret Mitchell

PICTURE CREDITS
*Artworks:* AntBits Illustration
*Bruce Coleman Collection*: (Mark Carwardine) 8–9. *Corbis*: (FLPA/Peter Reynolds) 15. *Image Bank*: (Cousteau Society) 13 below. *NHPA*: (A.N.T.) front cover, contents page, 5, 7 above, 12, 19, 21; (Andy Rouse) 23; (Douglas Dickins) 28; (Gerard Lacz) 6, 10, 18; (Norbert Wu) 13 above, 29 above; (Trevor McDonald) 9. *NOAA*: (National Marine Fisheries Service) 24. *Still Pictures*: (Horst Schafer) title page, 10–11; (Kelvin Aitken) 4, 16; (Mark Carwardine) 22; (Roland Seitre) 7 below, 20, 26, 29 below; (Yigal-Unep) 25.

Series created by Brown Partworks Limited.
Designed by Wilson Design Associates

Production by Omnipress,
Eastbourne, UK
Printed and bound in Dubai

2

# Contents

# Introduction

**Of the many creatures that live in the sea, dolphins are among the best known. There are lots of things about dolphins that will surprise you, though. Did you know that dolphins are not fish? In fact, humans are more closely related to dolphins than fish are.**

Dolphins and people are mammals. Mammals are animals with backbones that share certain features: Like you and me, dolphins breathe air, and dolphin babies are fed on their mother's milk. All mammals are warm-blooded and can keep their bodies at a steady temperature.

Also like us, dolphins love to

▼ *Some kinds of dolphins ride the bow waves of ships. This may be because swimming with the ship helps them save energy; but it seems they also do it just for fun, much the same as human surfers.*

## Dolphins at work

The U.S. Navy uses dolphins to find explosive mines, search for people lost at sea, and to carry tools to underwater sites. The U.S. Navy's Marine Mammal Program was set up to study how dolphins can swim so fast. The navy wanted to use this information to improve submarine, torpedo, and ship designs; but it soon realized that dolphins had many other useful skills. The navy's research has helped us understand how dolphins dive, swim, and echolocate.

▲ *The dusky dolphin is very acrobatic. It often "breaches," leaping high out of the water. One reason for doing this may be to look for feeding seabirds, which give away the presence of fish.*

socialize, and many dolphins live in groups several thousand strong. There are some things that dolphins can do that no person can, however. For a start, they spend most of their lives in the water. Also, in the same way that submarines navigate using sonar, dolphins use sound to "map" their surroundings and hunt with great accuracy. This ability is called echolocation.

# Dolphins at play

**Maybe you have seen dolphins in a marine park tossing a ball or leaping into the air? Those dolphins were trained to perform tricks on command. Yet wild dolphins do all those things and more without any training at all. In the ocean dolphins sometimes catch jellyfish and then use their tails to toss them into the air like a ball. Spinner dolphins leap out of the water and spin right around like a top.**

# Shape and size

**There are more than 30 different species (types) of dolphins, and they all look different. There are spotted dolphins and striped dolphins. Some are black and white, others are blue, and a few are pink.**

Dolphins also vary greatly in size, ranging from 4 ft (1.2m) to more than 13 ft (4m) long. All dolphins have sleek, streamlined bodies, however, and powerful tails divided into two lobes, or flukes. The dorsal (back) fin helps stop the dolphin from rolling over as it swims, though a few species have no dorsal fin. The flippers are used to steer.

Most dolphins have a noticeable snout, or beak. Dolphins cannot breathe through their mouths like us—that way only leads to the stomach.

*▼ This spotted dolphin's long snout is very noticeable, and its blowhole can be seen on the top of its head.*

Instead, they breathe through a hole on the top of their head called the blowhole. This hole is perfectly positioned to allow the dolphin to take a quick breath when it comes to the surface. The blowhole closes when the dolphin is underwater so the animal does not drown.

Dolphins have a thick layer of fat called blubber, which keeps their body warm. When they are very active, dolphins can even be in danger of overheating. The fins and flippers have no blubber, though, so they can be used to help control temperature.

To cool down, more warm blood flows around the fins and flippers, releasing heat into the water. To warm up, less blood flows through these parts, so more heat is kept inside the dolphin's body.

*▶ Spinner dolphins are the champion jumpers. They can leap 10 ft (3m) into the air and spin up to seven times.*

# Fast swimmers

The fastest dolphins reach speeds of more than 25 miles per hour (40km/h). The dolphin's tail beats up and down to propel the animal forward, but this alone is not enough to account for their fast speeds. Aeroplanes and ships are designed to reduce drag, and this is also true of dolphins. Drag is the resistance of a fluid to things moving through it. Dolphins do not have features that would disturb the smooth flow of water over the body, such as ear flaps, legs, or hair. Most importantly, though, the action of the tail creates a smooth-flowing layer of water over the body that greatly reduces drag.

▲ Dolphins swim so fast they can leap right out of the water and glide briefly through the air. This is called porpoising, and it lets dolphins save energy since they can take a short rest from swimming. These are dusky dolphins.

# Living together

**Nearly all dolphins live with other dolphins in a group called a school, herd, or pod. Open-ocean dolphins tend to live in large groups with more than 100 members and occasionally as many as 100,000 dolphins. Coastal and river dolphins mostly hang out alone or in much smaller groups of fewer than 20. Amazon river dolphins live singly or in pairs for most of the year.**

Large dolphin groups are made up of many smaller subgroups. In bottlenose dolphins these subgroups are generally of three types: nurseries made up of adult female dolphins and babies; juvenile dolphins; and adult males. Each of the smaller groups often numbers fewer than 25 dolphins. Adult males usually go around alone or with one or two other males. In striped

▼ *Dusky dolphins are rarely seen alone. Gatherings of up to 500 duskies meet in summer.*

▲ *Striped dolphins migrate in groups off the Japanese coast. They spend the summer in the North Pacific Ocean and the winter in the East China Sea.*

dolphins, however, subgroups of juveniles, mating adults, and nonmating adults form—so there is less separation between male and female dolphins.

The members of a subgroup usually stay the same, but the makeup of a large group changes more because subgroups come and go. Adult male subgroups can stay away from the larger group for months at a time, for example, or the larger group will just get together to feed or mate.

# Group ties

A dolphin group may contain several species of dolphins. Dolphins also swim with whales and tuna. Dolphins sometimes ride the bow waves of large whales. In parts of the Pacific Ocean groups of spotted dolphins play, rest, and mate during the day and feed at night. Spinner dolphins in the same waters rest at night and feed during the day. So there are always some dolphins on the lookout for predators.

# Getting along

**Why do dolphins live in groups? A good answer would be that they rely on each other's help to find food and watch for predators. Females also get help in raising their babies.**

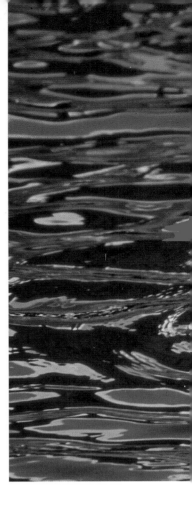

◄ *Dolphins blow bubbles to warn other dolphins of danger and as a warning sign to trespassing dolphins or other animals.*

In the vast oceans the large shoals of fish that dolphins seek out to eat can be far apart, so being part of a group makes it easier for a dolphin to find food.

Perhaps most importantly, living in a group gives protection. Dolphins have few predators, but those they have are fearsome: sharks and killer whales. A lone dolphin would be no match for a large shark, but several dolphins together can chase a shark away by butting and ramming it with their heads. Bottlenose dolphins have been known to gang up on harbour porpoises, killing them by biting and beating them. Perhaps the dolphins saw these smaller mammals as competitors or food.

Dolphins communicate with each other using squeaks, whistles, and groans. Air sacs linked to the airways of their blowhole make these sounds. Bottlenose dolphins have signature whistles; like names, they are unique to each dolphin. Dolphins also use body language a great deal. Breaching can tell other dolphins that there are fish to hunt, sharks to avoid, or dolphins in distress. Dolphins can also communicate their mood. An angry dolphin claps its jaws together, rams with its head, or smacks with its tail. Dolphins like to pet their friends, though, and use their head or mouth to caress other dolphins.

▲ *Members of a group hunt together, travel together, help each other out of trouble, and even play together. These bottlenose dolphins are showing affection.*

# Getting some shuteye

**Dolphins need to rest, but the ocean is a dangerous place. A fast-moving shark can easily catch a napping dolphin. Dolphins have solved this problem by letting only half their brain sleep at any one time and by living in groups, so they can take turns sleeping. Dolphins take lots of small naps of between 5 and 10 minutes throughout the day. Over a 24-hour period all these short sleeps can add up to between six and eight hours.**

# Finding food

**Dolphins are fast-swimming hunters, mainly of fish, squid, and octopus. Prey is swallowed whole, head first. Some dolphins feed at night, while others are more active in the early morning or late afternoon. Dolphins hunt for their food in a variety of ways.**

Dolphins living in shallow waters take fish off the seafloor. Common dolphins can catch fish in mid-air: they swim up underneath the fish, driving it out of water, and then leap up to snatch it out of the air. Nearer land bottlenose dolphins chase fish onto mudflats, then half-strand themselves to feed. Indo-Pacific humpback dolphins wriggle across mudbanks to catch their lunch. Around reefs and rocky coasts a dolphin might catch one fish, then use it as bait to tempt other fish hiding in crevices. Dolphins may even use very high-pitched clicks to stun their prey. In Shark Bay, Australia, bottlenose dolphins wear cone-shaped sponges on their snouts to protect them from stingrays while they hunt fish.

◄ *Most dolphins are expert divers. Risso's dolphins can stay under water for 30 minutes, and striped dolphins can reach depths of 655 ft (200m).*

# Cooperative feeding

Coastal and riverine dolphins and those that live on reefs hunt alone or in pairs, but in the ocean dolphins hunt together. A group of dolphins will herd the fish together, then take turns swimming through the tight shoal and eating their fill. Some will fluke the fish—slap them with their tail—as they pass to stun them. Commerson's dolphins form a half-circle and herd the fish against the shore before lunching. Off some West African coasts dolphins work with people to fish. The dolphins herd the fish into nets, then share the catch with the fishers.

▲ If dolphins work as a group, it is easier for them to herd fish together and make a killing.

The long dolphin snout is well suited to swiping at darting fish in the water. All dolphins have teeth; but their size and number vary according to diet. Some dolphins have only a few teeth; others have more than 100.

Risso's dolphins, which eat mainly squid, octopus, and cuttlefish, have only a few teeth at the front of their mouth, and none on the top jaw. Instead, they have rough patches that grip their soft-bodied prey.

▼ Dolphins that eat mostly fish have many sharp teeth to grip their slippery prey.

# To the rescue

**If a dusky dolphin screeches in a particular way, the other dolphins in its group know that a killer whale is in the area. In this and many other ways dolphins help protect each other.**

If a dolphin does come to harm, though, its companions will come to the rescue. Several dolphins will use their snouts or backs to keep the injured dolphin afloat with its blowhole out of the water. When members of a dolphin group strand themselves by swimming ashore, other dolphins will risk their lives trying to help their friends.

Dead baby dolphins have been found with fatal wounds inflicted by adult dolphins. It could be that male dolphins kill the young of certain females so that those females will mate with them;

▼ *The dolphin in the centre has been injured, and its two friends are nudging it back to the surface.*

## A helping hand

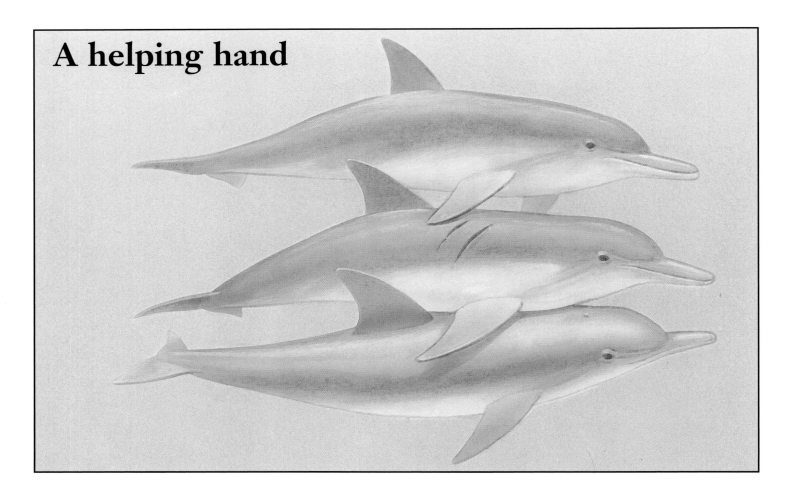

# Why do dolphins strand?

It is not clear why dolphins and whales sometimes become stranded on beaches. Here is one explanation: Cetaceans have tiny crystals of magnetite, a magnetic mineral, inside their heads. Dolphins probably use these crystals like internal compasses for detecting the Earth's magnetic field. However, sometimes they make mistakes, and whole schools of dolphins will swim ashore, probably as a result of taking a wrong turn a while before. That would explain why dolphins just rescued sometimes swim back onto the shore—they keep taking the wrong route.

▲ *If you find a stranded dolphin on the shore, seek expert help as quickly as possible. Sometimes a dolphin that appears dead will still be alive.*

perhaps females even kill their own young if times are hard. In captivity mothers and aunts have been seen drowning weak babies by holding them at the bottom of the pool. These cases seem to contradict our image of dolphins as kind, unselfish, and cooperative animals. Maybe, just like us, they are unselfish when it suits them; but under difficult circumstances, for example, when food is short, they have to use different tactics to survive. We still have much to learn about dolphin behaviour and society.

# The mating game

**Male dolphins are called bulls, and female dolphins are called cows. Bulls and cows are not easy for humans to tell apart, however, since their sex organs are hidden from view.**

The female's mammary glands and the male's penis are tucked away inside slits underneath the body near the anus. Males tend to be larger, but this is not always the case. Bottlenose dolphin males are ready to breed from 10 to 12 years old; but females can breed

## Kidnappers

During the mating season male bottlenose dolphins will work together to "kidnap" a female away from the group. They take turns feeding as the others guard her from other males. The female, who is not always unwilling, may be held captive for several weeks. The males do this so they can be sure of fathering offspring.

▶ As soon as the baby is born, it needs to surface to breathe. If the mother cannot help, one of her companions, called an "aunt," will guide the calf to the surface with her snout. The mother or aunt will support the calf while it takes its first breath.

◀ The spotted dolphin on the left looks a little larger than its friend, but that is the only clue telling us it is the male animal.

at a much younger age—between 5 and 12 years old. In some species the size of a dolphin is more important than its age.

Most dolphins breed at particular times of the year. Bottlenose dolphins, for example, breed between spring and autumn. During the mating season males fight over females and chase each other at top speed, showing off to the gathered females.

Babies, or calves, are born tail first after a year-long pregnancy. Twins and triplets are very rare but not unknown.

# Helping out

The underwater birth of a dolphin is a risky business for mother and calf. Labour can last for up to six hours, and sharks are attracted by blood, so the mother needs other dolphins to protect her. Pregnant bottlenose mums normally leave their group with a couple of females and go somewhere quiet nearby to give birth.

# Growing up

**For at least the first year of its life a young bottlenose dolphin will stay with its mother as part of a nursery. This nursery will contain several adult females, some with young and some without.**

The adult females have a lot to teach the young about how to survive at sea: how to hunt, echolocate, and how to interact with other dolphins. The fathers have little to do with their children, but there are many other females around who share the task of looking after the young. In large groups of dolphins nurseries travel in the middle of the group where they are protected from predators.

After one to two years the calf may leave the nursery and start hanging out with other dolphins

▼ *Calves ride in the slipstream of their mothers after birth. That means the young dolphin does not have to swim so hard to keep up.*

# Nursing babies

Dolphins feed on their mother's milk, often for more than a year. Dolphin milk is much richer than human milk, and this helps the baby grow quickly. Dolphins do not have lips, though, and they cannot suck since there is no air in their mouth, so how do they suckle? The mother dolphin ejects milk into the calf's mouth using muscles that squeeze the mammary glands. The calf just has to put its mouth in the right place. Bottlenose dolphins are suckled for at least a year. Dolphins in captivity have been suckled by other female dolphins after their mothers died.

of a similar age. Later on, females will return to the nursery as adults, while the males form their own more exclusive groups. Juvenile spotted dolphins sometimes join schools of spinner dolphins but return to groups of their own species when they become adults. Offspring often remain in touch with their mothers, though. Many return to visit mum after the birth of a brother or sister.

Dolphins also seem to form bonds with the dolphins they grew up with. The adult male bottlenose dolphins that hang out in groups could well have been in the same nursery as youngsters.

▲ *Dolphin mums can be strict: They will slap and scold their offspring if they misbehave or stray too far away. Dolphins have been seen flicking infants into the air with their heads, but who knows if this is a punishment or a reward!*

# Where dolphins live

**Dolphins live in all the world's oceans, though they are more common in tropical and temperate waters than in the coldest waters of the Arctic and Antarctic Oceans.**

Some dolphins live around coral reefs, which are found only in warm waters less than 100 ft (30m) deep. Clymene dolphins and rough-toothed dolphins are found in much deeper waters. Not all dolphins are sea creatures. Some live only in rivers, and others can live in fresh or salty water.

Many more dolphins range the open seas, often far from land. They swim and feed in the well-lit surface waters, some diving down to darker waters to hunt. A group might stay near the coast during the day, resting, playing, and mating, then move offshore at night to feed.

The type of place, or habitat, a dolphin lives in can affect what

◄ *Risso's dolphin has a wide distribution. It is found most commonly in warm waters in the Atlantic, Indian, and Pacific Oceans.*

the dolphin looks like. Coastal bottlenose dolphins tend to be smaller than ocean-going ones. The reasons for this are not known, but the differences can be so great that some experts think they are separate species. Compared to their marine relatives, river dolphins have very poor eyesight; but good eyesight would be wasted in the muddy waters they swim in.

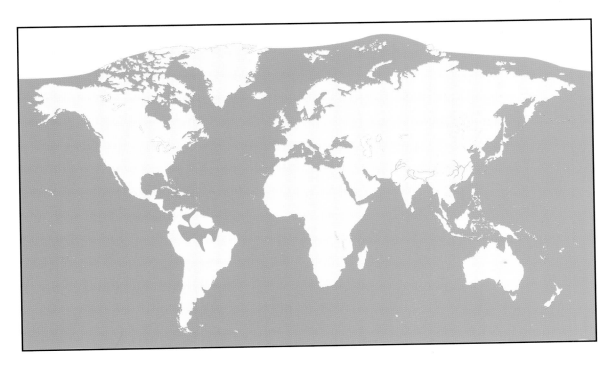

▲ A Hector's dolphin mum and her youngster. There are now fewer than 4,000 Hector's dolphins living in the wild.

◄ Map showing places in the world where dolphins can be found.

# Threatened habitats

Some dolphins are found almost all over the world, but others live in much smaller areas. Coasts and rivers are becoming more built up, increasing pollution and reducing dolphin habitats. Animals with limited ranges are at greater risk from habitat loss, pollution, and negative human contact. Hector's dolphin, for example, lives only in the coastal waters of New Zealand. Many Hector's dolphins have died in the gill nets that fishers set in these waters. The New Zealand government has now banned gill-net fishing where the dolphins live.

# ations

Dolphins belong to the group of marine mammals called cetaceans. Cetacean is the ancient Greek word for "sea monster," and the group includes the largest animal on Earth: the blue whale.

◄ **Killer whales are famous for their hunting techniques. In a few places they propel themselves onto the shore to snap up sea lion pups.**

Whales, dolphins, and porpoises are all cetaceans. Unlike other marine mammals such as seals, which haul themselves out of the water to breed, cetaceans spend all their lives in water.

The cetaceans include two groups of living whales: baleen whales and toothed whales. Baleen whales are the giants of the oceans. They have no teeth,

## What's in a name?

The term *dolphin* can refer to any member of the Delphinidae family. Usually, though, it is the smaller species that are called dolphins, and larger ones are called whales. Killer whales, or orcas, are the largest members of this family. They can grow up to 32 ft (10m) long. Because of their large size orcas are usually referred to as whales, not dolphins.

but large plates of baleen hang down from their upper jaw. Baleen is made from the same material as fingernails.

Toothed whales have teeth and are able to echolocate. The family of small toothed whales, or Delphinidae, includes killer whales, pilot whales, melon-headed whales, all marine dolphins, the Irrawaddy dolphin, and the humpbacked dolphins.

The ancestors of modern dolphins lived on land. They had fur, four legs, and no flippers. Over millions of years these early mammals evolved (changed gradually) into cetaceans. Perhaps the changes began when the land mammals started to feed on fish in coastal waters. They gradually began to live a more and more aquatic lifestyle until the land was abandoned altogether.

food. Thar ... swimming around in a spiral under a shoal of fish, all the time blowing out air from their blowholes. The bubbles form a net up to 150 ft (45m) across, which surrounds the fish. Then the humpbacks swim up through the shoal, swallowing their prey.

# Land-dwelling ancestors

Traces of the dolphin's land-dwelling ancestors are found in today's sleek sea creatures. Inside the dolphin's flippers are the bones of a hand, including three fingers. There are also tiny bones near the tail end that are not connected to the rest of the skeleton and serve no purpose: They are all that remains of the hind legs. The blowhole is all that remains of the ancestors' nostrils. As early dolphins evolved, the nostrils moved to the top of the head and became one hole. Baleen whales have two blowholes.

blowhole

flipper

# cholocation

**When we look at something, we are seeing reflected light. In a similar way dolphins can "see" with their ears.**

Dolphins listen to reflected sound to "see" objects. This is called echolocation. The dolphin sends out a series of clicks, often too high pitched for humans to hear. The sound waves bounce off objects in the water. The dolphin listens to the returning echoes of the clicks and uses this information to picture its surroundings.

When a dolphin has locked onto a fish, it sweeps the beam of sound over the animal by moving its head from side to side. As the dolphin gets nearer to its prey, the clicks get closer together and become much higher pitched. The dolphin can see much more with sound than we can with light because the echoes reveal the internal structure of things as well as their shape and size.

▼ *Without the ability to echolocate these dolphins would not be able to find fish and feed.*

## Hearing

Dolphins have no earflaps, but that does not mean they cannot hear. Instead, they have a tiny hole that leads to a well-developed inner ear. Most sounds reach the inner ear by passing easily through the blubber of the lower jaw, not this hole. Sound travels much faster through water than air, and dolphins can hear sounds from tens of miles away.

# The melon

The forehead of a dolphin generally bulges over the beak. This part of the head contains a fatty, oily organ called the melon. The melon acts like the lens of a camera, focusing the clicks into a powerful beam that can travel for up to 2,600 ft (800m). Another fat store in the lower jaw helps channel the returning echoes to the ear.

▲ A dolphin's melon gives its head a distinctive shape. For the dolphin this is far more important than just good looks.

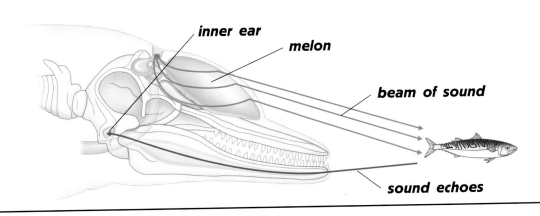

inner ear

melon

beam of sound

sound echoes

# River dolphins

**Not all dolphin species live in the oceans. Some of the largest rivers in the world are home to dolphins found nowhere else on Earth. The Ganges River in India and the Indus River in Pakistan are home to two very similar species. The boto, or Amazon river dolphin, is the largest of the river dolphins, measuring up to 8 ft (2.5m) long.**

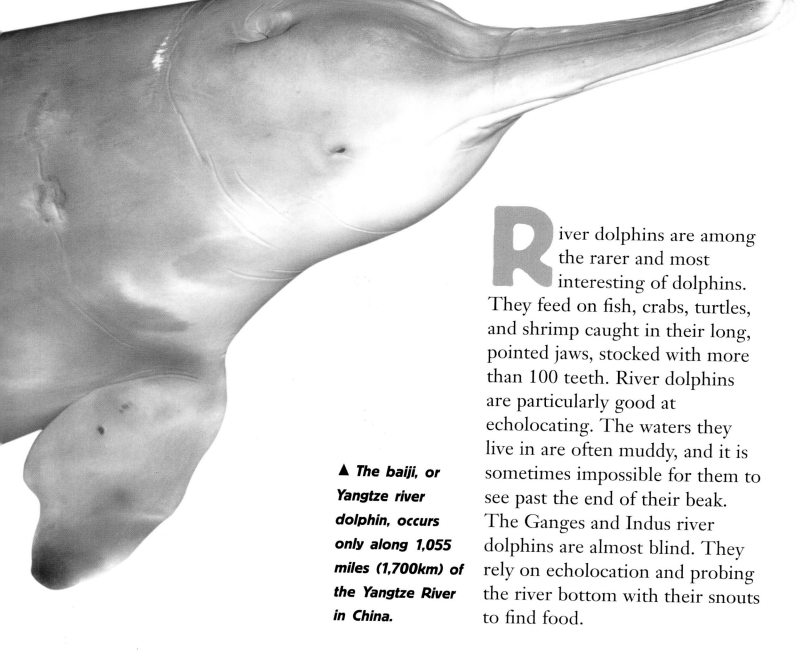

▲ *The baiji, or Yangtze river dolphin, occurs only along 1,055 miles (1,700km) of the Yangtze River in China.*

River dolphins are among the rarer and most interesting of dolphins. They feed on fish, crabs, turtles, and shrimp caught in their long, pointed jaws, stocked with more than 100 teeth. River dolphins are particularly good at echolocating. The waters they live in are often muddy, and it is sometimes impossible for them to see past the end of their beak. The Ganges and Indus river dolphins are almost blind. They rely on echolocation and probing the river bottom with their snouts to find food.

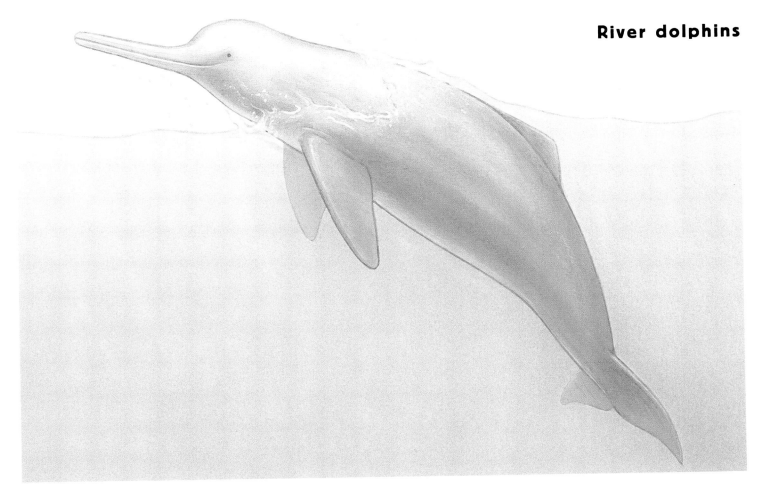

▲ *The boto, or Amazon river dolphin, lives singly or in small groups. Some are pink, and others are grey; their colour depends on age, location, and water clarity.*

River dolphins live in smaller groups than marine dolphins. The Ganges and Indus river dolphins live in pairs or alone. Other river dolphins live in groups of up to 15 members. With few natural predators (apart from people), river dolphins do not really need to live in large groups as marine dolphins do.

Like marine dolphins, though, the mothers still take good care of their young.

River dolphins do not just live in the rivers they are named after but also those that feed into it. One exception is the baiji, or Chinese river dolphin, which lives only in parts of the Yangtze River in China.

# Endangered species

River dolphins are at risk all over the world. River dolphins would normally migrate upriver in the rainy season, when the river is flooded. Dams have kept them from doing this in some rivers. Pollution has killed off many of the fish the river dolphins feed on, and they have to compete with people for those that remain. For such reasons there could be as few as 200 living baiji left in the wild. If their numbers get much lower, the population will never be able to recover.

# In captivity

**Keeping dolphins in captivity allows people to see these beautiful and intelligent animals in the flesh. It can also raise awareness of conservation issues.**

**W**ell-known and well-loved animals are more likely to attract the sort of attention that can force governments to protect them in the wild. If numbers of wild species do decline, it might be possible to use captive dolphins to restock the oceans. Keeping dolphins in captivity has also allowed scientists to study them closely. This can help dolphins as well as people: Scientists can use their knowledge to advise on how best to protect wild dolphins.

Some dolphinariums (places where dolphins are kept in captivity) do more harm than good, though. Not all parks tell their visitors how to treat their dolphins with respect: You must never touch a dolphin's blowhole,

◀ *This bottlenose dolphin knows it will be rewarded by its trainer if it leaps at the right time. Captive dolphins can become so dependent on their trainers that release back into the wild may be a major problem.*

► *Pacific whitesided dolphins performing in a dolphinarium.*

pat it on the sensitive forehead, or pull on its dorsal fin.

Sometimes, captive dolphins are released back into the wild. Perhaps a dolphinarium has been closed down, or maybe the release is part of a scientific study. If a release is carried out in the right way, the dolphins are taken back to where they were first captured. If all goes well, the released dolphins will be accepted into a local group. However, bad signs to watch for after a release are dolphins begging bathers for food or dolphins that are thin. These dolphins are still too dependent on people to survive on their own and should be recaptured and returned to health before the release is tried again.

# Training dolphins

**People train dolphins by praising the behaviour they want to see and ignoring things they do not want to see. As soon as the dolphin does something right, the trainer will blow a whistle or say "Good." The trainer will then do something the dolphin likes: feeding it a fish, rubbing it down, or playing with it.**

▼ *The bottlenose dolphin is the species most often kept in captivity. This type of dolphin seems to adjust well and is peaceful, playful, and eager to learn new tricks.*

# Further reading

**Dolphins**
by Kevin Holmes
(Children's Press, 1998).

**Dolphins**
by Casey Horton
(Benchmark Books, 1996).

**Dolphins**
by Erik Stoops and Jeffrey
Martin (Sterling
Publications, 1996).

**Dolphins' Days: the Life
and Times of the Spinner
Dolphin**
by Kenneth Norris
(W. W. Norton, 1991).

**Dolphins and Porpoises**
by Richard Ellis (Knopf,
1989).

**Dolphins and Porpoises:
a Worldwide Guide**
by Jean-Pierre Sylvestre
(Sterling Publications,
1993).

**Dolphins, Porpoises, and
Whales of the World**
by M. Klinowska
(IUCN, 1991).

**Sealife: A Complete
Guide to the Marine
Environment**
edited by Geoffrey Waller
(Pica Press, 1996).

**Whales and Dolphins**
by Anthony Martin
(Salamander Books, 1990).

**Whales, Dolphins, and
Porpoises**
by Mark Carwardine and
Martin Cann (Dorling
Kindersley, 1995).

## Web sites
www.acsonline.org
www.biscay-dolphin.org.uk
www.cetacea.org
www.iwaynet.com
www.wdcs.org

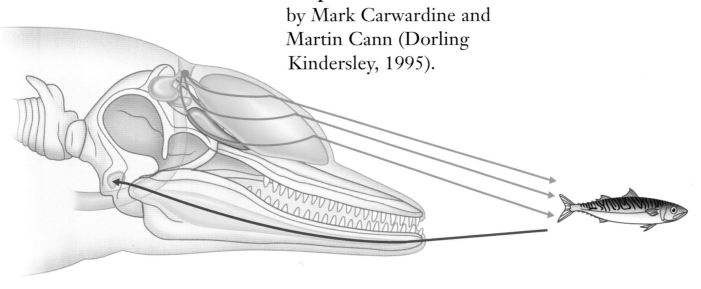

# Glossary

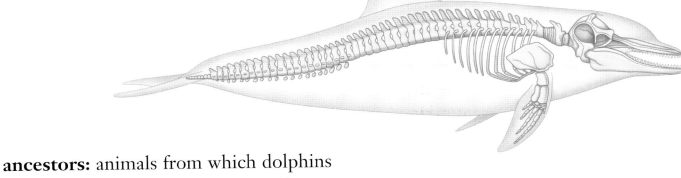

**ancestors:** animals from which dolphins have developed over many generations.

**baleen whale:** type of whale with a fringelike sieve growing from the upper jaw to extract krill from water.

**blowhole:** the nostril opening on a dolphin or whale's head that allows it to breathe.

**blubber:** layer of fat under a dolphin's skin that keeps it warm.

**breach:** leap clear of the water.

**calf:** baby cetacean that is still being nursed by its mother.

**cetacean:** one of a group of aquatic mammals including dolphins, whales, and porpoises.

**dorsal fin:** fin on the back of a dolphin.

**echolocation:** system used by dolphins to navigate and find food by sending out sounds and then "reading" the returning echoes.

**flukes:** the lobes on a whale's tail.

**krill:** small shrimplike crustaceans found in ocean waters.

**mammal:** a kind of animal that is warm-blooded and has a backbone. Female mammals have glands that produce milk to feed their young.

**mammary gland:** milk-secreting organ of female dolphins and other mammals.

**melon:** the organ on a dolphin's head that focuses the animal's clicking sounds into a powerful beam to echolocate.

**migration:** regular movement of animals from one region to another.

**nursery:** a group of female dolphins and their young.

**predator:** an animal that hunts and kills other animals for food.

**school:** a congregation of dolphins.

# Index